# Being a Leader

by Stuart Schwartz and Craig Conley

**Content Consultant:**
Robert J. Miller, Ph.D.
Associate Professor
Mankato State University

CAPSTONE
HIGH/LOW BOOKS
an imprint of Capstone Press

# CAPSTONE PRESS

818 North Willow Street • Mankato, MN 56001
http://www.capstone-press.com

*Library of Congress Cataloging-in-Publication Data*
Schwartz, Stuart, 1945-
    Being a leader/by Stuart Schwartz and Craig Conley
    p.cm. -- (Job skills)
    Includes bibliographical references and index.
    Summary: Introduces setting goals, learning how to resolve conflicts, and
considering all viewpoints in order to assume leadership on the job.
    ISBN 1-56065-715-4
    1. Career development--Juvenile literature. 2. Leadership--Juvenile literature.
[1. Career development. 2. Leadership.] I. Conley, Craig, 1965- . II. Title. III. Series:
Schwartz, Stuart, 1945- Job skills.
HF5381.S286 1998
650.1--dc21                                        97-53218
                                                        CIP
                                                        AC

**Photo credits:**
All photos by Dede Smith Photography

# Table of Contents

# Chapter 1

## Leaders on the Job

There are many kinds of leaders. A president leads a country. A coach leads a sports team. Groups need leaders to get things done.

Employers need leaders, too. An employer is a person or company that hires and pays workers. Employers hire people with strong leadership skills.

Being a leader takes special skills. Leaders must be dependable and fair. They set goals and solve problems. Good leaders listen to other workers. Leaders help other workers do their jobs.

For example, auto mechanics fix cars. A leader often decides which tasks each mechanic should perform. A leader may decide which cars to fix first. In this way, a leader may establish each worker's schedule for the day.

Many leaders at work are supervisors. A supervisor is a person who is in charge of other workers. But not all leaders are supervisors. All workers can be leaders if they have the skills.

**Being a leader takes special skills.**

# Chapter 2

## Setting Goals

All employers have goals. A goal is an objective that people try to accomplish. A restaurant owner's goal is to serve food of the best quality. A clothing store manager's goal is to sell a certain amount of clothing.

Leaders help employers choose goals. Leaders also help workers reach goals. For example, workers in a deli have a goal. Their goal is to sell 50 chicken sandwiches. A leader can help them reach their goal. The leader might help by recommending the chicken sandwiches to customers. A customer is a person who buys goods or services.

Leaders also set long-term goals. A long-term goal is an objective that takes a year or more to accomplish.

For example, a craft store manager wants to increase business by 15 percent in one year. The manager asks workers for suggestions. They decide to put ads in newspapers. They have special sales. Business increases. After a year, the store reaches the goal.

**Leaders set long-term goals.**

# Chapter 3

## *Being Dependable*

Leaders are dependable. Dependable people do what they say they will do. Employers value dependable people in the workplace.

Good leaders know that part of their job is helping other workers. They learn about the other workers' jobs. They offer to help when workers make mistakes or have trouble completing their work. Workers count on good leaders. They know these leaders are dependable.

Suppose a manager is preparing a company report. The manager needs to find sales records for the past three months. The manager turns to a salesperson who has been a leader in the past. The salesperson helps the manager find the records. The salesperson is dependable.

**Dependable people do what they say they will do.**

# Chapter 4

## Listening Skills

Good leaders have strong listening skills. They listen carefully to employers, workers, and customers. Listening helps leaders solve many problems.

For example, a receptionist answers telephones at a company. The receptionist tells a manager that angry customers are calling the company. The manager asks the receptionist why the customers are angry. Then the manager figures out how to satisfy the customers. The manager has helped the company and its customers by listening to a worker.

People also show how they are thinking or feeling with their bodies. This is called body language. For example, people shake their heads yes or no. People walk slowly if they are feeling tired. They walk quickly if they are excited. Good leaders pay attention to body language. A leader can learn how people are feeling by watching body language. This is another kind of listening.

**Good leaders listen to co-workers.**

# Chapter — 5

## *Motivating Others*

Good leaders know how to motivate workers. Motivate means to encourage others to do a good job. Workers who are motivated work hard. They try to reach goals. They often succeed with the help of leaders.

Leaders motivate people in many ways. Leaders praise workers when they have done a good job. Leaders make sure workers know how to do their jobs well. They help workers feel good about their jobs. Workers who feel good about their jobs are highly motivated.

Leaders motivate workers to improve. They help workers set deadlines and reach goals. Leaders may offer rewards to workers who complete projects on time.

People are motivated by different rewards. Some people work harder if they are rewarded with better pay. Some people work harder for extra time off. Leaders understand what motivates each worker.

**Good leaders know how to motivate workers.**

# Chapter — 6

## Understanding Differences

Good leaders understand that each worker is different. Workers come from different backgrounds. They have different knowledge and different ways of thinking. They may speak different languages. They work and solve problems in different ways. Good leaders treat each worker with respect.

Leaders know that differences make a team of workers strong. Each worker can contribute something special to the job. Contribute means to help get something done.

Leaders know that workers have different strengths and weaknesses. For example, one worker at a museum is good at putting together exhibits. Another worker is good at explaining exhibits to customers. A leader knows that each worker is strong in one area. The leader assigns tasks to each worker based on those strengths. The leader may also help each worker improve other tasks.

**Good leaders understand that workers are different.**

# Chapter 7

# Explaining Rules

Every employer has rules. Rules tell workers how to do their jobs. Some rules tell workers how they should treat each other. Other rules help workers stay safe in the workplace. Good workers follow workplace rules.

Leaders understand workplace rules. They know why rules help both employers and workers. They can explain rules to other workers. They tell workers why rules make sense.

For example, salespeople may ask why they cannot wear jeans while working in a store. A leader explains that customers expect salespeople to dress nicely. The customers might shop elsewhere if the salespeople wore jeans. This would hurt the store's business. Now the salespeople understand why they must obey this rule.

**Leaders explain rules to other workers.**

# Chapter 8

# *Changing the Rules*

Some rules do not work well. Workers know that some rules cause problems. They question the rules or make suggestions to change them.

Leaders listen to workers. They learn about problems caused by workplace rules. They think about how to solve these problems. Then they explain their ideas to supervisors or employers. Their ideas may include changing workplace rules.

For example, a group of workers might work 40 hours of overtime in a month. Workplace rules allow this much overtime. The workers are tired. They begin making mistakes at work. A worker sees the mistakes.

The worker tells a supervisor that the workers are tired. The worker shows the supervisor the mistakes.

The supervisor makes a new rule. Workers can work only 15 hours of overtime in a month. The worker has shown leadership by telling a supervisor about a problem.

**Good workers tell supervisors about problems.**

# Chapter — 9

# *Being Fair*

Workers have the right to be treated fairly. Good leaders are fair. Good leaders do not treat some workers better than others. Leaders also make sure workers treat each other fairly.

For example, workers at a grocery store might have to mop the floor. The workers make one worker do the mopping every day. A leader sees that this is unfair. The leader asks a supervisor to change work assignments. Now all workers must take turns mopping the floor.

Being fair also means treating workers well. Good leaders do not set unfair goals. For example, mechanics might be able to fix an average of 10 cars each per day. The supervisor could ask one mechanic to fix 25 cars each day. But this would not be fair. Good leaders choose goals that are fair.

**Good leaders treat workers fairly.**

# Chapter 10

## Solving Problems

Leaders solve problems on the job. They find out what the problems are. They ask questions. They listen to the ideas and suggestions of other workers.

Good leaders work to find solutions. A solution is a way to fix a problem. Leaders talk to others about solutions. They consider all the possible solutions. They choose the one they think will work best.

For example, a clerk in a toy store notices that fewer customers are coming to the store. The clerk talks to other workers and to customers. They all say that the store does not have enough new toys. The clerk tells the store's manager. But the manager says the store does not have enough space for new toys.

The clerk asks others for suggestions. The clerk thinks about possible solutions. The clerk finds a way to reorganize the space in the store. Now the store can offer more new toys. The manager likes the idea. The clerk has shown leadership by solving a problem.

**Leaders solve problems on the job.**

# Chapter ── 11

## Dealing with Emergencies

Leaders know what to do in emergencies. An emergency is a sudden and risky situation. Emergencies may keep workers from doing their jobs. For example, the electricity may go out. A roof might leak. Machines might break. A worker might get hurt or become sick.

Good leaders stay calm during emergencies. This helps them make good decisions. Good leaders know employers' rules for emergencies. They know what steps to take. They make sure workers are safe. Leaders can give first aid if needed. First aid is care given to someone who is sick or hurt.

For example, a machine in a factory might stop working. A worker knows a broken machine can hurt people. First the worker shuts off the machine. The worker makes sure that other workers are safe. Then the worker calls someone who knows how to fix the machine. The worker has shown leadership by handling the emergency.

**Leaders know what to do in emergencies.**

# Chapter 12

# Leadership Skills and You

Good leaders have useful leadership skills. Anyone can become a leader. You can practice leadership skills on the job. Start by being a good worker. Know how to do your job well and safely. Be dependable and fair. Try to do your best work each day.

You can also work on other leadership skills. Help other workers do their best. Know your employer's goals and help reach those goals. Listen to other workers. Look for ways to solve problems.

Ask your supervisor to help you think of ways to improve your leadership skills. Ask about classes you could take. Many schools and companies offer classes on leadership.

Being a good leader will help you succeed at work. It might help you get a raise. A raise is an increase in pay. Being a good leader might also help you earn a promotion. A promotion is a better, higher-paying job. Leadership also helps you feel good about yourself and your skills.

**You can practice leadership skills on the job.**

# Words to Know

**body language** (BOD-ee LANG-gwij)—the movements people use that show what they are thinking or feeling

**emergency** (i-MUR-juhn-see)—a sudden and risky situation

**employer** (em-PLOI-ur)—a person or company that hires and pays workers

**goal** (GOHL)—an objective that people try to accomplish

**motivate** (MOH-tuh-vate)—to encourage others to do a good job

**promotion** (pruh-MOH-shun)—a better, higher-paying job

**raise** (RAYZ)—an increase in pay

**supervisor** (SOO-pur-vye-zur)—a person who is in charge of other workers

# *To Learn More*

**Parker, Julie**. *High Performance through Leadership*. New York: Rosen Publishing Group, 1996.

**Schwartz, Stuart and Craig Conley**. *Exploring Job Skills*. Looking at Work. Mankato, Minn.: Capstone High/Low Books, 1998.

**Schwartz, Stuart and Craig Conley**. *Improving Work Habits*. Life Skills. Mankato, Minn.: Capstone High/Low Books, 1998.

# Useful Addresses

**Canada WorkInfoNet**
Asticou Training Center
Room 2161
241 Boulevard Cite des Jeunes
Hull, Quebec K1A 0M7
Canada

**Employment and Training Administration**
200 Constitution Avenue NW
Room N-4700
Washington, DC 20210

**Training Information Source, Inc.**
1424 South Clayton Street
Suite 200
Denver, CO 80210

# Internet Sites

**America's Job Bank**
http://www.ajb.dni.us

**Career Development Information**
http://www.training-info.com/

**Dare to Lead**
http://www.dynamicleadership.com/leader.html

**Skills Most in Demand by Employers**
http://www.utoronto.ca/career/skills.htm

# *Index*